BLAST THROUGH THE PAST!

AN ADVENTUROUS HISTORY OF PIRATES

Izzi Howell

W

FRANKLIN WATTS
LONDON • SYDNEY

Franklin Watts
First published in Great Britain in 2016 by The Watts Publishing Group

Copyright © The Watts Publishing Group 2016

Produced for Franklin Watts by
White-Thomson Publishing Ltd
www.wtpub.co.uk

Credits
Series Editor: Izzi Howell
Series Designer: Rocket Design (East Anglia) Ltd
Series Consultant: Philip Parker

The publisher would like to thank the following for permission to reproduce their pictures:
Alamy: Granger, NYC. 8, Lebrecht Music and Arts Photo Library 11t, 15, 19r and 27, North Wind
Picture Archives 17, 21, 24 and 25, AF archive/FILM COMPANY COLUMBIA PICTURES 29;
Dreamstime: Alexander Babich 10; Getty: Bettmann 7; iStock: duncan1890 14 and 16, javarman3
22l; Mary Evans Picture Library: 13 and 23; Shutterstock: Syrytsyna Tetiana cover b, samantha
grandy 4-5, Dudchik 6, Arne Bramsen 9, igor.stevanovic 11b, Marzolino 12t, Jubal Harshaw 12bl,
Patryk Kosmider 18, Jesus Cervantes 19l, maodoltee 22r, Sorbis 26, Nightman1965 28; Stefan
Chabluk 31; Wikimedia: Joseph Nicholls cover t, Heritage Auctions 12br, Open Clip Art Library
20t and c, Bastianow 20b.
All design elements from Shutterstock.

Every attempt has been made to clear copyright. Should there be any inadvertent omission
please apply to the publisher for rectification.

ISBN 978 1 4451 4939 4

Printed in China

MIX
Paper from
responsible sources
FSC® C104740

FSC
www.fsc.org

Words in **bold** appear in the glossary on pages 30 and 31.

Franklin Watts
An imprint of
Hachette Children's Group
Part of The Watts Publishing Group
Carmelite House
50 Victoria Embankment
London EC4Y 0DZ

An Hachette UK Company
www.hachette.co.uk

www.franklinwatts.co.uk

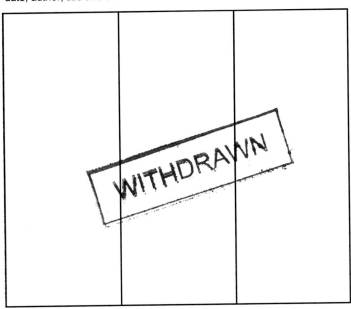

CONTENTS

PIRATES THROUGH HISTORY

As long as there have been ships and trade, pirates have attacked and stolen from them. The word pirate comes from an ancient Greek word, meaning someone who attacks ships, but different pirates have made their money in many ways – raiding villages, ransoming hostages and selling captives as slaves.

While some might see pirates as brave explorers who stole gold from wealthy European countries (who had actually stolen the treasure first themselves!), they were also cruel thieves who terrorised the seas and killed thousands of innocent people. Read on to find out about some of the most famous pirates of all time.

This timeline shows you the names, nationalities and dates of the people mentioned in this book.

Queen Teuta
of Illyria
(Balkans) ●
3rd century BCE

Julius Caesar
(Italy) ○
100–44 BCE

NORTH
AMERICA

ATLANTIC
OCEAN

SOUTH
AMERICA

Controlled a
pirate army of
8,000 men

Ching Shih
(China) ●
1775–1844

Anne Bonny
(Ireland) ○
c.1702–1782

Christopher
Moody
(England)
1694–1722

Mary Read
(England)
c.1690–1721

Calico Jack
Rackham
(England)
c.1682–1720

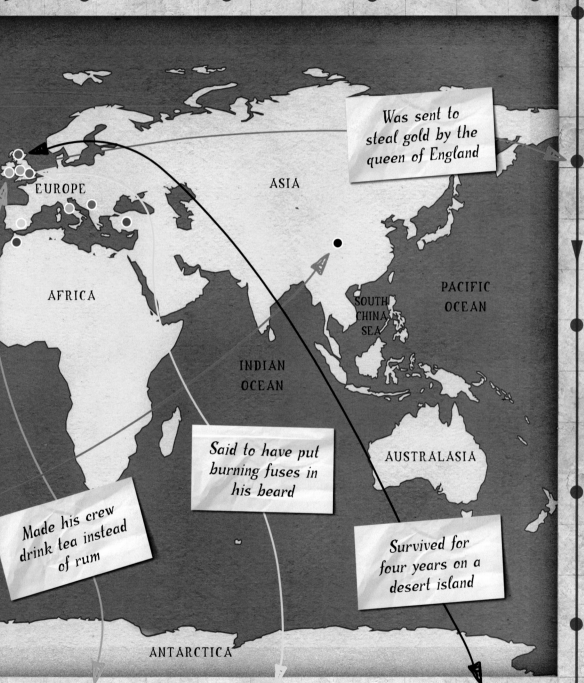

Christopher
Columbus
(Italy)
CE c.1451–1506

Aruj Reis
(Ottoman
Empire)
CE c.1474–1518

Khizr Reis
(Ottoman
Empire)
c.1478–1546

Sayyida al Hurra
(Spain/Morocco)
1485–c.1542

Queen
Elizabeth I
(England)
1533–1603

Sir Francis
Drake
(England)
1540–1596

Henry Morgan
(Wales)
1635–1688

William Kidd
(Scotland)
1645–1701

Henry Every
(England)
1659–1696

Bartholemew
Roberts
(Wales)
1682–1722

Blackbeard
(Edward Teach)
(England)
c.1680–1718

Alexander
Selkirk
(Scotland)
1676–1721

ASIA

EUROPE

AFRICA

PACIFIC
OCEAN

SOUTH
CHINA
SEA

INDIAN
OCEAN

AUSTRALASIA

ANTARCTICA

Was sent to
steal gold by the
queen of England

Said to have put
burning fuses in
his beard

Made his crew
drink tea instead
of rum

Survived for
four years on a
desert island

5

MEDITERRANEAN MARAUDERS

Ancient Mediterranean civilisations often transported goods by ship as it was much speedier than moving stuff across land. Pesky pirates preyed on these traders as they sailed along the coastline.

Coastal thieves

Early pirates had to sail close to the shore as their ships weren't strong enough for choppy open water and they had no maps or tools for navigating at sea. They hid their ships in **inlets** while waiting for their next victim to pass by. Any trade ship was a target, even ships from their local area. They also raided coastal villages for supplies, and slaves to row their **galleys**.

MUST BE ABLE TO:
attack accurately

At first, pirates chased their victims until they could jump on board and fight at close range. After the invention of the metal **ram**, pirates only had to get close enough to punch a hole in the side of the other boat – no easy feat when travelling at speed! Damaged boats would sink quickly, so pirates swiped their spoils as fast as possible!

Pirates would often strike just as traders were unloading their goods from their galleys.

For many years, small groups of pirates working alone were considered an inevitable part of life at sea. However, this all changed in the 3rd century BCE, when Queen Teuta of Illyria (modern-day Balkans) gave permission to large numbers of pirates to attack **Romans** and **Greeks**. These **privateers** made the seas so dangerous that the Romans invaded Illyria and Teuta surrendered.

HAVE YOU GOT WHAT IT TAKES?
RANSOMER

TOP SKILL: Demanding top dollar

Brainy Mediterranean pirates quickly learned that you could make more money by stealing people and holding them to ransom, than by selling stolen goods. They targeted important people, as they knew they could expect a sky-high pay-off for their release.

As a young man, the Roman politician Julius Caesar was captured by pirates from Cicilia (modern-day Turkey) and held to ransom for a small sum. Caesar was so offended by this mini ransom that he persuaded the pirates to double it. After it was paid, Caesar hunted down the pirates and got his own back by having them killed.

Do you know who I am?

VICIOUS VIKINGS

Northern Europe was also terrorised by pirates, such as the fierce **Viking** raiders that attacked along the coasts in the 8th to 10th centuries CE.

Across the sea

The Vikings were excellent sailors and navigators, travelling from **Scandinavia** to attack seaside **monasteries** and villages in Scotland, Ireland, England and France. Monasteries were their top targets as they were jam~packed with valuable gold objects and books. They also nicked cattle, tools and food from villages.

MUST BE ABLE TO:
sail along the shore

Viking longships were perfect for raiding as they could sail in the shallow water near coasts and along rivers. This allowed the Vikings to sneak up close to their target before launching a surprise attack. In the Viking language, the word 'viking' may have even meant 'someone who lurks in a bay'!

In open water, longships were powered by the wind, but close to shore, the Vikings had to get out their paddles and row!

Early Vikings were **pagans** so they had no problem stealing from a **Christian** church or slaughtering a **monk**. Vikings believed that as long as their loot was won in battle, it didn't count as stealing. After a few years of hit-and-run attacks, the Vikings came back to seize villages and land. They expanded their territory and set up new bases for future attacks.

HAVE YOU GOT WHAT IT TAKES?
TRADER

TOP SKILL: Reselling stolen goods

The Vikings took some of their ill-gotten gains back to Scandinavia. They melted down gold and silver and made them into new objects. They also traded stolen goods along Viking **trade routes**, which stretched as far east as Russia. Rulers sometimes paid the Vikings money to stay away, but flashing the cash often encouraged raiders to come back for more!

Monks and villagers lived in terror of surprise Viking attacks, with shiploads of warriors brandishing deadly weapons.

9

REVENGE OF THE CORSAIRS

In the 16th century, piracy returned to the Mediterranean in a big way thanks to corsairs – **Muslim** pirates who were based along the coast of North Africa. Corsairs targeted Christian trade ships and stole sailors to sell into the **slave trade**.

Getting even

In the first half of the 16th century, tensions ran high between Christians and Muslims around the Mediterranean. The Christian rulers of Spain kicked out many Spanish Muslims, whose families had lived there for centuries. These people fled to North Africa and parts of the Muslim-ruled **Ottoman Empire**. Privateers from both sides worked to disrupt trade routes, but it was the corsairs based in North Africa who dominated the Mediterranean.

steal a slave

As galleys became bigger and heavier to support the weight of new weapons, such as cannons, they became harder to row. So, corsairs stole people to do the exhausting work of rowing for them! Having a large crew also meant that it was easy for them to overpower enemy crews.

Pirates weren't the only ones to get extra help rowing. Many countries forced criminals to row **navy** galleys – a fitting punishment for a convicted pirate!

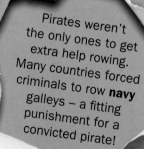

10

NAME: Aruj Reis (c.1474–1518) and Khizr Reis (c.1478–1546)

NATIONALITY: Ottoman

AKA: The Barbarossa brothers

ACHIEVEMENTS: Older brother Aruj began the family business of piracy, working as a privateer against Christian knights who were hired as privateers by Christian countries to disrupt Ottoman trade. He built up a mega **fleet** of stolen ships and used his power to conquer the city of Algiers, in Algeria, which he turned into a base for pirates. After Aruj was killed by the Spanish, his younger brother took over as chief pirate and continued to terrorise Christians across the eastern Mediterranean Sea.

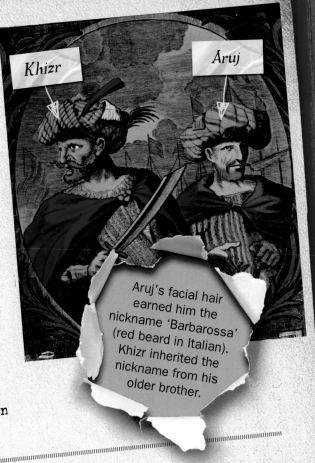

Khizr *Aruj*

Aruj's facial hair earned him the nickname 'Barbarossa' (red beard in Italian). Khizr inherited the nickname from his older brother.

NAME: Sayyida al Hurra (1485–c.1542)

NATIONALITY: Spanish/Moroccan

AKA: Queen of the pirates

ACHIEVEMENTS: Sayyida was deeply affected when Christians forced her Spanish Muslim family to move to Morocco. Her friendship with the Barbarossa brothers inspired her to gather a fleet of ships and start attacking Christian trade routes. Sayyida never set foot on a pirate ship, but she instructed her pirate fleet with such success that she soon controlled most of the piracy in the western Mediterranean. She used the money stolen from Christian ships to rebuild Moroccan cities that had been destroyed by the Spanish and to help Spanish Muslim **refugees** start new lives.

Malta – base for Christian knights who acted as privateers

Spain

Algiers

Algeria

Morocco

PAYING FOR PIRATES

After the Italian explorer Christopher Columbus reached the continent of North America in 1492, Spain sent conquistadors (conquerors) to Central and South America. The conquistadors seized huge areas of land, which became part of the **Spanish Empire** in the early 16th century.

Stealing from the Spanish

The Spanish conquistadors stole a vast amount of gold and silver from Central and South American civilisations, such as the **Aztecs**. This treasure was taken to the islands and mainland around the Caribbean Sea, known as the **Spanish Main**, before being transported by ship back to Spain.

The Spanish made their stolen gold and silver into coins. Pirates could use Spanish coins in many places as they were used as a trade **currency** across the world.

Spanish Main

Atlantic Ocean

Over 100 ships laden with treasure sailed from the Spanish Main to Europe every year in the early 16th century.

Spanish gold doubloon coins

These silver Spanish coins were nicknamed 'pieces of eight' for their value of eight reales – a unit of Spanish currency.

12

As news spread of Spain's wealth, the rulers of some European countries, such as France, England and Holland, sent privateers to raid Spanish **galleons** as they made their way across the Atlantic Ocean and bring them back a share of the gold. This was technically legal if a country was at war with Spain, which handily happened quite frequently!

PITILESS PIRATES

NAME: Sir Francis Drake (c.1540–1596)

NATIONALITY: English

AKA: Pirate with permission

ACHIEVEMENTS: Drake was a privateer who raided his way all around the world with the permission of his number one fan, Queen Elizabeth I of England. He stole so much Spanish gold that he couldn't even carry it all in his ship, the *Golden Hind*. He returned to England with millions of pounds worth of treasure to the delight of Queen Elizabeth, who knighted him for his service.

HE SAID WHAT?

'It isn't that life ashore is distasteful to me. But life at sea is better.'

Sir Francis Drake

MUST BE ABLE TO:
get a letter of marque

Privateers needed an official licence, known as a **letter of marque**, to show that they had permission from their country to attack and raid. Otherwise, they were plain old pirates! After their mission was complete, privateers were supposed to return their ship and give up all of their ill-gotten gains to their king or queen.

Queen Elizabeth I knighted Francis Drake on his ship, the *Golden Hind*, for his excellent work as a privateer.

Well done you naughty boy!

MEET THE CREW

Not every privateer wanted to give up their hard-earned treasure to the king or queen. Many privateers became pirates, attacking merchant ships around the Caribbean without permission and keeping all the gold for themselves.

Pirates were allowed to swear and drink on board, especially after a successful raid!

Crew 'mates'

Although most pirates lived outside the law, life on a pirate ship was quite fair. All of the crew shared rations and loot equally, although the captain got slightly more! They voted on how and when to attack and decided on a set of rules that everyone on board would follow, known as the pirate articles.

HAVE YOU GOT WHAT IT TAKES?
RULEMAKER

PERSONALITY PROFILE: Good as gold

The pirate articles helped to keep troublesome pirates in line. Most ships banned gambling (which usually led to arguments), fighting between crew members and helping yourself to treasure. Henry Morgan's pirate crew valued their beauty sleep, so their articles stated that all lights had to be out by 8pm!

If a pirate broke the rules, or did something even worse, such as abandoning ship during battle, they faced a seriously nasty punishment from their crewmates. Pirate punishments included being marooned, **flogged** or even killed (no one was ever made to walk the plank ~ this idea comes from pirate novels and films!). If pirates were caught by the law, they were locked up for life or executed, with their rotting bodies left in cages as a warning to other pirates.

HAVE YOU GOT WHAT IT TAKES?

MALE IMPERSONATOR

MUST HAVE: A decent fake beard

Women weren't generally allowed on pirate ships, as they were believed to bring bad luck, but some female pirates managed to bend this rule by dressing up as men. By cutting their hair and wearing loose clothes, Anne Bonny and Mary Read fought as part of Calico Jack Rackham's crew for years without raising much suspicion.

MUST BE ABLE TO:

survive a marooning

Marooning was the awful punishment of being abandoned on an island with some food, water and a pistol. Marooned pirates went mad from the loneliness and thirst and burned to a crisp in the hot sun. However, it was possible to survive a marooning. Alexander Selkirk lasted four years on an island in the South Pacific Ocean by eating wild turnips!

SHE SAID WHAT?

'Had you fought like a man, you need not have been hang'd like a dog.'

said to Rackham after he had been captured by pirate hunters

Anne Bonny

Oh no, Anne, I've lost my fake beard!

Calico Jack knew the women's true identities and even had a relationship with Anne. When pirate hunters caught Jack's crew, the women managed to escaped hanging, as they were both pregnant.

ATTACK!

As soon as a ship was sighted, pirates sprung into action. They needed to guess the strength of the crew and the value of their cargo before deciding to attack, as a pirate ship had no chance against an armoured navy ship.

Grappling hook

Pirates in pursuit

As pirate ships were smaller than trade galleons, they could travel much faster. Pirate ships often chased their enemies for several hours, slowly growing close enough to call for the other ship to surrender. Meanwhile, the pirate crew prepared for battle in case the other ship was up for a fight!

Musket

Some sneaky pirates lured their victims in by pretending to be regular ships. Once their targets were close to their ship, they raised their pirate flag and attacked!

MUST BE ABLE TO:

board an enemy ship

If a ship refused to surrender, pirates would open fire with their cannons, being careful not to do too much damage in case the ship sank before they stole their goodies! They threw grenades (bottles filled with gunpowder) and shot at the enemy sailors with **muskets** so that the deck of the ship would be clear for boarding. Finally, the pirates used grappling hooks to pull the ships close enough together to hop across.

Cutlass →

In a confusion of gunfire, explosions and smoke, pirates leapt on board the enemy ship. They used axes and cutlasses to fight at close range and break through the decks to find scaredy~cat captains hiding in their cabins. Most of the time, sailors were no match for battle~hardened, cut-throat pirates. After the pirates had won, they grabbed what they could ~ treasure, new crew members and even the ship!

HAVE YOU GOT WHAT IT TAKES?
SHIP'S 'SURGEON'

MUST HAVE: A sharp saw

The stereotypes of pirates with wooden legs and eyepatches are 100 per cent true. Although pirates usually won their battles, they didn't escape unharmed and their wounds often became infected. Other pirates were given the task of sawing off infected limbs, as there were rarely doctors on board. The upside was that the captain compensated pirates up to 600 pieces of eight for every limb lost in battle, as agreed in the pirate articles.

PITILESS ⚔ PIRATES

NAME: Blackbeard (Edward Teach) (c.1680–1718)

NATIONALITY: English

AKA: Terror of the seas

ACHIEVEMENTS: Fighting with a musket, two swords, six pistols and many knives, Blackbeard was a killing machine. To scare his enemies further, he is said to have tied burning fuses to his beard to surround himself with smoke. His reputation was so fearsome that most sailors surrendered as soon as they saw his flag. Blackbeard didn't go down without a fight and only died after being shot five times and sliced twenty times with a sword.

Er, water please!

Blackbeard's ship, *Queen Anne's Revenge*, was armed with 40 cannons. There are rumours that Blackbeard drank rum mixed with cannon gunpowder, which he set alight before drinking.

LIFE AT SEA

In between battles, life on a pirate ship was pretty domestic. Being equal meant that everyone had to lend a hand with the chores, and busy pirates had less time to get into trouble!

HAVE YOU GOT WHAT IT TAKES?
ATHLETE

MUST HAVE: Guns of steel

As well as being in fighting form for battle, pirates needed to be agile and strong to take care of their ship. Muscular arms helped pirates climb up the **rigging** to change sails and work the pump that drained dirty water from the **bilge** at the bottom of the ship.

This is a modern reconstruction of a 17th century pirate ship.

rigging

Keeping clean

To keep their boat ship-shape, pirates mended ropes and torn sails, cleaned their weapons and hunted down the rats that munched on the crew's supplies. Luckily, there were usually far more men on board than necessary, in case an extra crew was needed to run a stolen ship, so there were plenty of hands on deck to help out!

bilge

When they weren't fighting or doing chores, pirates entertained themselves by singing, dancing or napping. It was probably hard to get a good night's sleep in a hammock strung up on the deck in the middle of a storm!

HAVE YOU GOT WHAT IT TAKES?

**** COOK ****

MUST HAVE: A strong stomach

Pirates didn't have fridges to store fresh food, so they lived on salted pork and hard, bug-infested biscuits. They had a limited amount of fresh water, so most drank beer or rum instead. Peckish pirates could turn to the sea for fresh food, such as fish or sea turtle eggs.

PITILESS 🛡 PIRATES

NAME: Bartholemew Roberts (1682–1722)

NATIONALITY: Welsh

AKA: Boring Bart

ACHIEVEMENTS: Bartholemew earned himself a reputation as a cruel and ruthless pirate, taking over 470 ships during his career. He didn't allow himself or his crew to cut loose, even in their free time. He banned smoking and alcohol on his ship, preferring tea instead, and held church services every Sunday!

HE SAID WHAT?

'A merry life and a short one shall be my motto.'

Bartholemew Roberts

Pirate ships were stocked with food and water so that the pirates could survive for months at sea without having to return to land.

Bartholemew captured a fleet of ships off the coast of West Africa. Pirates operated all around the world, not just in the Caribbean (see page 22).

19

LAND AHOY!

Pirates spent much of their time at sea looking for treasure, but once they were rolling in gold, they came back to land to spend their ill-gotten gains!

Target acquired

Finding a ship to attack in the ocean was no easy task. A map showing the trade routes of Spanish ships was one of the most valuable items a pirate could steal. The Spanish sent their trade ships in **convoy** with warships to protect them, so pirates twiddled their thumbs until a ship got separated from the pack. While they were hunting for a target, pirate ships didn't fly pirate flags so as not to attract attention.

Pirates only raised their flags once a target had been spotted, in the hope that the ship might surrender instead of fight.

PIRATE FLAGS

This is the flag of Calico Jack Rackham. Pirate flags are also known as 'Jolly Rogers'.

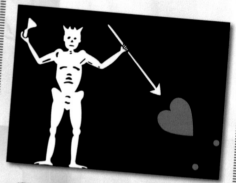

This is rumoured to be the flag of Blackbeard. The skeleton is spearing a heart while offering a drink to the devil.

Not all pirate flags were black. Christopher Moody's red Jolly Roger showed an hourglass with wings to show his victims that their time alive was running out.

On land, pirates headed to dodgy cities, where they could restock supplies and spend their gold without attracting attention. The Caribbean island of Tortuga was a popular pirate hangout as it was divided between the French and the English, who were too busy fighting each other to pay attention to the pirates.

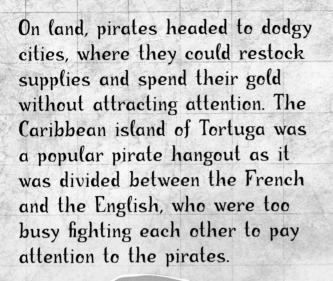

Hic, 'nother rum Cap'n?

Oooo-Argh!

Pirates drank beer and rum on board, but nothing compared to the amount they put away when they got to shore.

THE PIRATE ROUND

As European countries cracked down on piracy in the Caribbean, pirates looked for new targets and struck gold with the trade ships that travelled through the Indian Ocean.

Round and round

Caribbean pirates made their way to the Indian Ocean via the pirate round. They travelled across the Atlantic and down around the southern tip of Africa, before stopping for supplies in Madagascar. Once they had a ship full of loot, they headed back to the Caribbean.

Barnacles

HAVE YOU GOT WHAT IT TAKES?
BARNACLE BRUSHER

TOP SKILL: Keeping things ship-shape

Islands such as Madagascar were the ideal spot for ship spring-cleaning. Pirates grounded their ships at high tide so that they could repair holes and scrape sharp **barnacles** off the bottom. The weight of the barnacles weighed down the ship and made it slower, so a clean ship helped pirates chase down their victims at sea.

This gravestone in Madagascar marks the resting place of an unlucky pirate. Madagascar was rumoured to be the spot of a pirate haven called Libertatia.

The round trip known as the 'pirate round'

ATLANTIC OCEAN

Africa

INDIAN OCEAN

Caribbean

Madagascar

The best hunting grounds for trade ships were off the coasts of Yemen or India. It was easy for pirates to prey on ships carrying silk, jewels and precious metals, as no nearby countries provided powerful navies to protect them. When Henry Every became the richest pirate in the world after ransacking a 25-ship-convoy, European countries sent pirate hunters to get things under control.

PITILESS PIRATES

NAME: William Kidd (1645-1700)

NATIONALITY: Scottish

KNOWN FOR: Lying about loot

ACHIEVEMENTS: Although William was originally sent to the Indian Ocean to catch pirates, he was pushed into piracy after his crew nearly **mutinied.** He attacked the very ships he was sent to protect and tried to pass off his spoils as confiscated treasure from other pirates. The English government didn't buy William's story and he was executed.

There are rumours that William Kidd buried his treasure in the Caribbean, but this is unlikely. Pirates probably spent their gold as soon as they came by it to stop other pirates nicking it for themselves!

Surely this is deep enough?

THE AGE OF THE RANSOM

In the 18th century, pirates in the Mediterranean embraced the ultimate get-rich-quick trick ~ holding ships to ransom. The days of raiding ships for chests of treasure were nearly over.

Making money

Clever corsairs loved ransoming ships, as getting paid cash in hand for doing nothing was much easier than attacking a ship and trying to find a buyer for stolen treasure. They attacked and ransomed so many ships that countries created special ransom funds. Some European governments even paid the pirates not to attack their ships in the first place!

The Ottoman rulers supported the corsairs as they got a cut of the pirates' ransom money! They often negotiated with foreign governments on behalf of the pirates.

24

Europeans had just about accepted Mediterranean piracy as inevitable when the USA became its own country at the end of the 18th century. American ships often sailed in the Mediterranean, but they didn't have enough money to pay off the pirates so they said no to the ransoms and sent warships to protect their trade ships instead. As other European countries copied the Americans and stopped paying the pirates, the corsairs slowly faded away in the 19th century.

MUST BE ABLE TO:

outsail a pirate

In the past, pirates had been able to chase down heavy, slow trade ships, but this changed after traders and navies started using speedy steamships in the 1830s. Pirates in wind-powered ships no longer had the advantage and slowly got left behind.

The corsairs didn't go down without a fight. In 1803, they captured a hugely valuable American warship. The Americans snuck back on board and burned their ship so that it wouldn't remain in the hands of the pirates.

JUNK FLEETS

In the 19th century, the South China Sea was teeming with small **junk** ships transporting goods and people. This attracted hoards of treasure~hungry pirates.

Junk attack

Merchant junk ships were small wind~powered boats, but in the wrong hands they became dangerous weapons. Pirates filled the stolen boats with rows of cannons so that they could attack their victims from a distance.

Cannonball

This is a modern junk ship. They are still used in some parts of China and southeast Asia today.

Chinese pirate lords controlled huge fleets of ships that sailed and attacked together. Some fleets were made up of hundreds of ships and thousands of bloodthirsty pirates. People in coastal villages were so scared of pirate raids that they paid the pirate lords to stay away.

PITILESS PIRATES

NAME: Ching Shih (1775–1844)

NATIONALITY: Chinese

KNOWN FOR: Pirate power

ACHIEVEMENTS: After Ching's pirate husband died, she took his massive fleet and made it even bigger, eventually controlling 1,800 armed ships and 8,000 men. Her pirate army was so powerful and terrifying that the Chinese, British and Dutch navies tried to take her down … but none succeeded. Finally, Ching accepted a peace deal in which all of her pirates were forgiven and she was allowed to retire from piracy with all of her ill-gotten gains!

Ching Shih fought with a large curved cutlass and wore women's clothes. She didn't disguise herself as a man, unlike other female pirates.

MODERN PIRATES

Today, piracy is luckily quite rare, but there are still a few pirates that operate off the east coast of Africa and in the South China Sea.

For ransom

Unlike pirates of the past, who took to the seas for a life of excitement and sparkly treasure, modern pirates are usually men from **deprived** communities who work for ransom money. Their main targets are slow cargo ships and tourist boats, which they capture and hold hostage until the ransom is received. Some pirates also steal liquid fuel, which they can sell on to unsuspecting sailors.

MUST BE ABLE TO:

embrace technology

Modern pirates use the latest technology to organise their attacks. Speedboats allow them to whizz up alongside slow boats, while smartphones and social media help them to communicate with each other, recruit new pirates and find investors who will sponsor their raids.

Gadgets such as night vision goggles are crucial during night-time attacks.

Cargo ships are huge compared to the boats used by the pirates.

Typical pirate speedboat

54° 25' 30" N – 18° 39' 15" E

Although modern piracy is uncommon, it can get out of hand if not controlled. Many governments no longer pay ransom money, which discourages pirates from carrying out the raids in the first place. Cargo ships travelling through areas of piracy have started to carry weapons and plan for pirate attacks. However, piracy will probably never end as long as people are desperate to make money by any means possible.

HAVE YOU GOT WHAT IT TAKES?
SECURITY GUARD

TOP SKILL: Protection from pirates

For years, armed pirates used ladders to climb on board cargo ships, while the ship's tiny, unarmed crew sat and watched helplessly. Now, these ships are armed with tons of anti-pirate features, such as electric fences around the ship, hoses, sound guns, armed guards, lasers and jets that spray smelly liquid and foam on the deck!

In the film *Captain Phillips*, which was based on the true story of a Somali pirate attack on a cargo ship, the ship's crew used hoses to try to stop the pirates from coming on board.

GLOSSARY

barnacle – a very small sea animal with a shell that clings to rocks and the bottoms of boats

BCE – The letters 'BCE' stand for 'before common era'. They refer to dates before CE 1.

bilge – the bottom inside part of a ship where dirty water collects

CE – The letters 'CE' stand for 'common era'. They refer to dates from CE 1.

Christian – describes someone who follows the religion based on the Bible and the teachings of Jesus Christ

convoy – a group of ships that travel together

currency – the units of money used in a country or area

deprived – describes someone who doesn't have enough money, food or resources to live a normal life

fleet – a group of ships

flog – to hit someone many times as a punishment

galleon – a large, wind-powered ship used from the 15th century to the 18th century

galley – a long, low ship that was rowed by prisoners or slaves

inlet – a narrow strip of water that goes from the sea into the land

junk – a Chinese ship with square sails

letter of marque – a letter issued by the king or queen that gave a man permission to attack and steal from enemy ships

monastery – a building where a group of religious men (monks) live

monk – a man who belongs to a religious group and lives apart from other people

musket – a gun with a long barrel that was used in the past

Muslim – describes someone who believes in the religion of Islam

mutiny – when a group of sailors refuses to take orders from their leader and tries to take control

navy – an armed force of ships and sailors who fight wars at sea, usually belonging to one country

pagan – someone who does not follow one of the main world religions, such as Christianity

privateer – someone who had permission from their country to act as a pirate

ram – a part of a boat that sticks out and is used to break through the sides of other ships

refugee – someone who has been forced to leave their country

rigging – the ropes that support a ship's sails

Scandinavia – an area that includes modern-day Sweden, Norway and Denmark

slave trade – the buying and selling of slaves

Spanish Main – a name for the area of the Caribbean and the coastline of the Gulf of Mexico when it was controlled by the Spanish in the 16th to 19th centuries

trade route – a route used by people buying and selling goods

EMPIRES OF THE WORLD

VIKINGS
(CE 700–1100)
– a group of people originally from Scandinavia that conquered land across northern Europe and the north Atlantic, creating a Viking empire.

ROMANS
(735 BCE–CE 476)
– a highly developed civilisation that built a vast empire. The Roman Empire was at its greatest extent around CE 117.

GREEKS
(750–30 BCE)
– an advanced Mediterranean civilisation that studied science, maths and medicine.

Legend:
- Vikings
- Aztecs
- Greeks
- Spanish (c.1600)
- Ottoman
- Romans

AZTECS
(CE 1100–1521) – a group of people that ruled over most of Mexico and Central America before the arrival of the conquistadors.

OTTOMAN
(CE 1301–1922)
– an empire that started in Turkey and spread across much of southeast Europe, west Asia and North Africa.

SPANISH
(CE 1492–1898)
– an empire that reached its peak in the 16th and 17th centuries and controlled large areas of South America, North America and Asia.

INDEX

Further information

http://www.dkfindout.com/uk/history/pirates/
Learn about pirate adventures and how pirates were punished.

http://www.nationalgeographic.com/pirates/bbeard.html
Read the story of Blackbeard, one of the most terrifying pirates of all time.

http://mocomi.com/history-of-pirates/
Find out tons of fun facts about pirates.

Every effort has been made by the Publishers to ensure that the websites in this book are suitable for children, that they are of the highest educational value, and that they contain no inappropriate or offensive material. However, because of the nature of the Internet, it is impossible to guarantee that the contents of these sites will not be altered. We strongly advise that Internet access is supervised by a responsible adult.